THE ESSENTIALS OF
BOWLING

THE ESSENTIALS OF BOWLING
APPROACHING THE PERFECT GAME

SECOND EDITION

STEVEN FELEGE

King Pin Publishing   Lake City, Pennsylvania

The Essentials of Bowling
Approaching the Perfect Game

By Steven Felege

Second edition

Published by:
King Pin Publishing
P.O. Box 22
Fairview, Pennsylvania 16415

Library of Congress Control Number: 2012933160

ISBN: 978-0-9849721-0-4 softcover

Design and composition: www.dmargulis.com

Illustrations by Elizabeth Watasin, www.a-girlstudio.com

Manufactured in the United States of America

First printing, March 2012

Contents

To Beth, Chris, Lynn, and Luke

Acknowledgments

Dreams rarely come true without the help and encouragement of others. This book is no exception. I would like to express my sincerest appreciation to a few of my many friends and acquaintances, without whom *The Essentials of Bowling* probably would not exist except as an entry on my "bucket list."

Luke Curlett, my friend and mentor, once said to me, "You can learn more from bad bowlers than you can from the good ones 'cuz there's more of 'em, and the good ones— they ain't talkin'." Rest in peace, my friend. I miss you!

Beth Peck walked into Suburban Bowling Lanes back in April of 1976. I bowled a 650 series that night—the highest set of my career at that time. She never walked out of my life. Beth, I cannot thank you enough for all that you have done to make this, and so many of my other dreams come true! I still love you, boss (3–9, +1)! The adventure continues!

The last time my son, Chris, and I bowled together was in the Junior–Senior tournament at Suburban Family Bowling Center. He was ten years old, *and we won*! It was the proudest day of my bowling career. Thanks for all the memories, Buddy.

When I coached my daughter, Lynn, in the junior league, she took a word of advice from me, put it to good use, and started beating the boys. I still remember that advice. I think it's the only time she actually listened to me. Just kidding, doctor. I'm proud of you!

Without the guidance of Carol Joyce (former English teacher, close personal friend), each chapter would have been one long run-on sentence. Thanks for pointing that out!

Everyone should have a friend like Gene Chiappazzi (master of the known universe). When I mentioned that I was working on this book, he didn't hesitate to volunteer his time and expertise. His photography produced the images used to create the artwork seen in this manual. Thanks for always being there, Gene!

Linda Hoover is a local hall-of-fame bowler, three-time certified bowling instructor, and a true ambassador of the game of bowling. Linda said, "Steve, when you get this published, I want two copies." When a competitor of Linda's caliber said that, I knew this book had to happen. Thank you, Linda!

Carol Mancini is my very best friend in California. She is the editor and publisher of the *California Bowling News*. She has bowled in many different countries, and her name appears in three halls of fame. After reading my manuscript, she said, "Anybody who bowls needs to read this book!" Of course she then told me how to make it even better. Carol, I cannot thank you enough.

Of course, turning this dream into a reality required more than encouragement. It needed a team quite different from any I had ever dealt with before. A sincere thank you to Dick Margulis, who edited the manuscript, designed the book, and managed the project; Elizabeth Watasin, who had the unenviable task of illustrating the delivery of a bowling ball to my exacting specifications and did so with patience, talent, and creativity; and Sharyn Mathews, who proofread the typeset pages.

Introduction

There is a big difference between knowing *what* you want and knowing *how to get* what you want. All bowlers *want* to get better. This book teaches you *how* to get better, nothing more, nothing less. Your improvement relies on learning a few universal principles of successful technique and then adjusting your skills to follow them.

The Essentials of Bowling is *not* just another "Bowling: A to Z" book. It is a clear and concise manual that will allow you to take the abilities you already possess and improve them. Because it is primarily for someone who already bowls, I assume that you, the reader, have a basic knowledge of bowling terminology and technique. Even if you do not—if you are a beginner, in other words—this book will serve you well as a platform on which to base the game you are about to develop.

Many bowling books and bowling instructors teach the same standard techniques that have been taught for generations. These may be the very skills you are using. The fact that you are looking at this book proves that you sense there must be a better way, and you are right! The techniques in this modest manual are based on sound and rational logic rather than strict adherence to traditional teachings.

The Essentials of Bowling is formatted to make it an easy-to-use reference source. It is a common sense look at the game and the skills it requires. It introduces you to the importance of the *basic skills* and then describes exactly how to perform them *properly*. These descriptions, if combined, make up less than one full page of normal text, making it easy for you to incorporate what you are about to learn into a two- to three-second delivery.

The techniques described in this book are tried and true, easy to learn, and effective. Some of these techniques differ from traditional teachings. For this reason, each chapter ends with a discussion and explanation of each element of that particular skill. It is not necessary for you to read the "Discussion" sections. Their only purpose is to help you understand why these techniques work and need to be practiced exactly as described to allow you to achieve your full potential.

Another aim of this book is to save you time and money as you seek to improve your game. For most people, both are limited resources. Of the four basic skills you are about to relearn, three can be practiced and easily mastered *at home*, in front of a mirror! You will be able to practice wherever and whenever you want.

I wish you a lifetime of better bowling!

NOTE This book is written and illustrated in "right hand." Translation into "left hand" is unnecessary (except where noted) because the techniques you are about to learn are universal.

CHAPTER 1

A True Story

Thirty-two weeks ago, nobody could have predicted that the season would end like this. Here at Eastway Bowling Lanes, the championship of the Sunrisers' League is coming down to the last frame of the last game of the last week of the season.

The Ten-Pins are leading the Six-Pack by nineteen pins. Mark and Lenny, the last two bowlers, step up to the *approach*, that fifteen-foot stage on which they will perform their final act of this season. Both are capable bowlers, which is why they anchor their respective teams. To say that the two men don't like each other very much is an understatement. One loves the game; one loves to win. This difference has fueled a growing rivalry over the years.

Lenny, a short, aging overhead crane operator is on lane 1 for the Six-Pack. He cradles his ball with both hands and takes a step back, signaling his opponent to go first, a standard protocol for this game.

Mark, a brash, swaggering, young former marine, steps up onto the approach. He glances up at the electronic scoreboard and, seeing his enviable position, can't resist taunting his nemesis. "All I have to do here is throw a strike and I close you guys out!" He grins as he prepares himself for battle once more. He's been locked on to the pocket all game long. He feels his confidence surge. Victory is assured!

Lenny remains calm and focused. He inserts his fingers into his ball, stretches his hand around it until his thumb goes in smoothly, and then reverses the process as he patiently awaits Mark's delivery.

Up on the approach, Mark takes some extra time to savor the moment. All eyes are on him, and he loves it! In his mind, he pictures the pins exploding as his ball crashes mercilessly through them. He can't wait to rub Lenny's nose in the fact that he beat the hated Six-Pack when it counted most—when it was for the championship. Now, he imagines his drill sergeant standing behind him, barking out his marching orders.

"Acquire your target, soldier!"

Target acquired, sir! he says to himself.

"You may fire when ready!" the imaginary officer yells.

Ready! Slowly he slides his left foot forward and takes the first step toward his target.

Aim! As he approaches the foul line, he winds himself up like a coiled spring.

Fire! Mark unleashes another of his thunderous shots. The ball hits the alley with a loud *thunk* and churns its way down the lane. He watches with satisfaction as the ball rolls over its intended spot and begins its long, powerful arc toward the pocket. He smiles broadly as he waits for the resounding *crash!* that will accompany ten pitiful pins reeling into the pit, bringing him the glory that he craves.

Maybe he waited too long. Maybe he put too much rotation on the ball. Maybe he set it down on the lane too soon. Maybe he had slowed his delivery down just a smidge. Maybe…! It doesn't matter. For whatever reason, all he can do now is watch as, at the last moment, his ball dives up onto the headpin and slices cleanly through the array of pins.

Maybe I'll get lucky, he thinks, as he watches pins roll lazily around on the deck. *Maybe, just maybe* … , but today there is no luck. "Oh, come on!" he yells at the pins as though they are alive and subject to his commands. As he turns away from them, he puts his hands on his hips and hangs his head in disgust.

"These lanes *suck!*" he growls. He looks up and glares at Lenny as the pinsetter comes down and picks up his 4–6 split, sweeps the deck clear, and then resets them with tormenting precision.

"Win by whatever means necessary, soldier!" he hears his sergeant command. He switches his strategy to psychological warfare. Mark believes that he can get into Lenny's head, mess with his mind, and cause him to make a bad shot. He can still take credit for the win when the Ten-Pins claim the trophies. "You still need to strike out to win!" he snarls at Lenny as he steps off the approach to await the return of his ball. Mark doesn't know Lenny very well.

Lenny didn't see the results of Mark's shot. He doesn't hear Mark tell him that he still needs to strike out, and he doesn't even glance up at the scoreboard. The diminutive elder statesman of the league, Lenny is physically no match for Mark, but mentally, it's a different story.

The Lucky Little Leprechaun, as he is affectionately called, steps up onto the approach and places his feet in exactly the same position he has been placing them for the entire game. He looks up and faces his target, the second arrow, making sure that his shoulders are squared to it. Next, he removes his thumb from the hole and raises the ball to his lips. He always does this; it's part of his routine. To most people, it appears that he is giving his ball a kiss, but in reality he is putting a puff of air into the thumbhole. The little bit of added moisture gives him a better grip and keeps the ball from slipping off his hand too early.

Lenny places his thumb back into the ball and, supporting it with both hands, lowers it to his waist. He takes a deep breath as he begins the next phase of his routine, the chant. *Stance!* he thinks firmly. At this moment, he is no longer merely Lenny, a five foot four inch, 150-pound, blue-collar worker who just can't wait to retire. He is now a *bowler*!

In his mind, he quickly runs through his stance checklist:

- Face target
- Weight on one foot
- Shoulder dipped down
- Elbow tight to my side
- Forearm pointed at the second arrow
- Palm under the ball

He is ready! Without hesitation, he confidently takes his first step forward.

Pushaway! Smoothly and deliberately, he begins to push the ball down and away from himself, directing it toward the second arrow. He concentrates on keeping his palm under the ball until his arm is perfectly straight.

Armswing! Using *no* muscle power at all, Lenny allows his arm to simply drop, while maintaining his firm grip on the ball. He continues to focus on keeping his hand under and then behind the ball as it swings like a pendulum.

Keep the backswing low, he reminds himself. The last thing he wants right now is a high backswing. Not only would it throw off his timing, but it would also twist his shoulders around and take his armswing off his target line. He applies the brakes. The backswing comes to a halt, and the ball begins to move forward. His hand is still positioned behind the ball.

As Lenny's left foot begins its short slide toward the foul line, the ball nears his ankle and he gives himself one last silent command: *Release!* He loosens his grip. As the ball rolls cleanly off his thumb, he lofts it out onto the lane with his fingers.

A mere 2.4 seconds have elapsed since he began to take the first step in his approach. He hears a *thud* as the ball lands and heads directly for its target. *That's a good shot*, he calmly thinks. It's as emotional as bowler Lenny allows himself to get.

There is nothing flashy in Lenny's delivery. There is nothing fancy in his footwork—no awesome display of power. His whole approach is simple but produces devastating results. His ball rolls true and crushes the pocket! Ten in the pit, as they say.

"Yeah!" yells one of his teammates. "Nice shot, Lenny!" says another. "C'mon man, one more!" pipes another as he slaps him on the back. Just a few short minutes ago, they were all watching what they thought was a whole season slipping away. Maybe it still was, but at least now they felt that there was a chance, and they were all glad that it was Lenny up there giving them that chance. What a difference 2.4 seconds can make!

As he waits for his ball to return, Lenny steps back off the approach to allow Mark to shoot for his spare without distraction. It isn't necessary but shows respect and good sportsmanship toward his opponent. He stays focused by keeping his head down and staring at the spot on the approach where he will again plant his feet. He barely hears a faraway *click* as Mark's second shot picks off the six pin.

An open frame is *not* how he had planned to end his season, but Mark isn't quite done yet! "These lanes suck!" he snorts again. He stays up on the approach to wait for his ball. He is stalling, hoping to break Lenny's concentration, a tactic similar to icing a field goal kicker at the end of a football game by calling a time-out.

Still staring at the approach, Lenny steps up and picks his ball from the return.

"You still need two more strikes to win, Leprechaun!" taunts Mark.

Lenny plants his feet. He blows into the thumbhole and repeats his mantra, *Stance! … pushaway*! … *armswing! … release! … WHAM!* Ten more pins in the pit! His teammates breathe a sigh of relief, smile, and pump their fists. "C'mon Lenny, one more time!" someone says, but he doesn't hear them. Up on the approach, he looks at the new rack of pins the machine has prepared for him and says to himself, "Focus! It's just another shot."

Ka-chunk! Lenny's ball announces its arrival. He picks it up for his last shot of the season. "It's just another shot …" he repeats to himself as he plants his feet once again, exactly as before.

Standing on the tiled floor, Mark has positioned himself right behind Lenny. He is still holding his ball, mindlessly wiping the day's oil and grime from it as he waits for his enemy's final shot. "Nine to tie!" he chirps and then adds, "Eight … youuuuuu loooooooose!"

Lenny ignores him. He has completed his stance checklist and begins his approach. *Pushaway*! he repeats as he moves the ball toward its target.

THUD! The sound is so loud that Lenny not only hears it—he *feels* it!

Lenny's concentration is destroyed! His armswing goes out of alignment, and his wrist position collapses. Instantly, he knows he has to abort this shot! He has to start over, but one of the hardest things for a bowler to do is to stop in the middle of an approach. He squeezes the ball as hard as he can and manages to hang on to it! He swings it up to his chest just as his left foot slides over the foul line.

Red lights flash and bells ring, signaling that the foul line has been violated. Lenny angrily sets his ball back down on the return and asks, "What … the … hell … was … that!?

He sees Mark stooping over to pick up the bowling ball he had just dropped "accidentally."

Mark looks up to see little Lenny standing over him with his hands on his hips. The two men stare at each other for a second, and then Mark breaks into a grin. "Ooooooops!" he says impishly and then adds, "You fouled, man! We win!" He picks up his ball, turns away from Lenny, and then sticks his thumb into it and quickly pulls it back out, creating a resounding *pop!* Ignoring every protocol of sportsmanship, he does it again—*pop!*—and again—*pop!*

The rules state that "a foul occurs whenever a bowler crosses the foul line as he delivers the ball." Since Lenny never delivered his ball, no foul had occurred, and he knows it. Mark knows it too, but he hates to lose, and feeble mind games are now the only shots he has left.

Lenny is a very good bowler, but he is an even better coach. For over three decades, he has been teaching kids and adults what is important in bowling and what is not. Mark and his pitiful actions are *not* important.

Technique!—that's important! Good technique and luck create good results, but one can never rely on luck; just ask Mark.

There is always a heckler in his classes who will invariably chime in with, "I'd rather be lucky than good, coach!" Lenny has a standard response to this. He calls it simply "lesson number 1," and it is this: "Luck is when preparation meets opportunity."

It is time for him to listen to his own advice. He is prepared, and this is certainly an opportunity! Without further hesitation, he picks up his ball. He places the big toe of his right foot on the third dot at the back of the approach. He screws his fingers into the ball as tightly as he can, brings it up to his lips, and blows gently into the thumbhole. He stares at his target, the second arrow from the right gutter.

He takes a deep breath to relax as he lowers the ball and faces his target.

Pop!

Stance!

- *Shoulders squared with target … check.*
- *All my weight on my right foot … check.*
- *Right shoulder dipped down … check.*
- *Elbow tight to my side … check.*
- *Forearm pointed straight at the second arrow … check.*
- *Palm under the ball … check.*

Pop!

Confidently, Lenny takes his first step toward the foul line.

Pushaway! He deliberately pushes the ball directly toward his target, leaving virtually *no* room for error. He focuses on keeping his palm under the ball as he feels his arm straighten until the elbow locks …

Pop!

Armswing! He shifts his attention to avoiding the use of muscle power as his arm begins its pendulum-like swing. *Keep the backswing low,* he reminds himself. He begins to apply the brakes and start the forward part of the swing. *Hand behind the ball … check!* he thinks as he begins his slide toward the foul line and the ball nears his ankle.

Pop!

Release! He feels the ball roll cleanly off of his thumb and lofts it out onto the lane, his fingers once again guiding it toward the second arrow. *That's a good shot,* he thinks. *At least I made a good shot.*

Lenny gets down on one knee. There is nothing he can do now but watch. It's a good shot, but is it good enough? Will the ball hit the pocket or jump up on the headpin like Mark's ball did? Even if it hits the pocket, will it leave a ten pin or, worse yet, leave two pins standing to mock him as the 4–6 split had just done to his opponent?

He watches his ball as it closes in on the pins; it looks good. It looks *real good*! "Come … onnnn." *Wham!* "Pack your bag, Mark! We'll see you next year!"

Exciting, nail biting matches like this happen every day in league play. When you get into one, are you Lenny or Mark? Let's face it that we all want to be Lenny. We all want to be the one who can come through in a clutch situation, perform under pressure, and carry the team to victory.

There was a reason that Lenny was successful. He knew *how* to bowl, and that's what this book is about—to teach *you* how to bowl like a champion!

CHAPTER 2

The Education of Lenny

Was Lenny just lucky, or did he know something that Mark didn't? To be sure, he knew *many* things that Mark did not, the most important of which was *how to think like a bowler*!

He knew better than to complain about the lane conditions; they were the same for both teams. He understood that the game was really about reading those conditions and adjusting to them.

He knew to ignore Mark's antics. Nothing his opponent ever did was important. He wasn't bowling against Mark; he was bowling against *the pins*.

He knew that bowling was much more than just throwing a ball at the pins and hoping for the best. Bowling balls are *delivered*, not *thrown*!

He knew to ignore the scores. They were a distraction. They never mattered until the game was over, and they were merely a reflection of how well he had adjusted his skills to suit the lanes. He knew that high scores didn't happen just because he wished for them; he had to make them happen.

He knew to ignore the fact that this match was for the league championship and that as the cleanup bowler, his teammates were relying on him for the win.

He knew that in order to win, he had to give his team a chance to win. That meant nothing more than *making good shots*.

He knew that *making good shots* meant focusing on his technique and *nothing else*!

Lenny knew *technique.*

Lenny first picked up a bowling ball at the age of twelve and immediately fell in love with the game despite being lousy at it (he scored 29). He had watched another bowler practicing on the lane beside him roll one strike after another and wondered how he did that. The other bowler made it look so easy. Learning to bowl like "that guy" became a passion for him.

The pursuit of this passion, to become as good as "that guy," became a lifelong quest. He soon discovered that anyone who even owned a bowling ball had advice to offer about the game. Sadly, he also realized that in many cases the random bits of information he gleaned from one source would conflict with what another source had said. His challenge evolved from learning all that he could about his sport to separating what really worked from what did not.

Now, at the age of fifty-three, he only bowled once a week but carried an extremely respectable 213 average. Yes, he definitely knew something Mark did not. He knew how to bowl. He knew what to focus on and what to ignore. He knew how to give his team a chance to win. Where Mark counted on natural athletic ability, constant practice, and emotion, Lenny relied on experience, education, a thoughtful strategy, and discipline.

Over four decades of bowling had taught Lenny that the *only* thing that mattered on the approach was *technique*: repeatable skills that produced dead-on accuracy. To his own surprise, his years of studying the sport had resulted in the discovery of a set of principles that govern successful technique. He refers to them as "the absolute truths of bowling."

An absolute truth is a concept that applies to everyone whether small, medium, or large; young or old; male or female; right-handed, or left-handed. These truths are as follows:

1. Bowling is a game of *skill*, not power.
2. What *you* do on the approach determines what the *ball* does on the lane.
3. The ball travels a *line* toward the pins.

Lenny's father, a contractor, had taught him that "a strong house is built on a strong foundation." When he decided to rebuild his game from scratch, these three principles became the foundation for that game. Using them as the basis for separating good advice from mindless drivel, he developed and choreographed a *system* of simple, well-defined fluid skills that he applied *every time* he stepped up onto the approach. These skills are:

1. The **S**tance
2. The **P**ushaway
3. The **A**rmswing
4. The **RE**lease.

This **SPARE** system works for Lenny, but it will also work for *any* bowler. A closer look at Lenny's system reveals why.

About absolute truth number 1, skill versus power: Many bowlers never achieve their true scoring potential because they rely on their strength to throw the ball as hard as possible. They think that more power will knock down more pins. That may sound logical, but it's only partially true for a number of reasons. Here are just a few of them:

1. You want to deliver *strikes* because strings of strikes produce high scores. That means rolling a very heavy ball

a very long way (sixty feet) into a very small pocket over and over again. That requires accuracy and precision. Power alone cannot accomplish this because muscles are unreliable. They react differently each time you use them. When they are cold, they respond one way; once warmed up, they act another way. They tighten up; they loosen up; they get tired and sore. You get the idea.

Trying to develop a power game without first learning the *basic skills* is like trying to learn to drive a race car without using the steering wheel. All the power in the world is worthless if you can't make it behave! Whatever strength you have is enough; you must develop skills that *direct* your strength, not vice versa.

2. During the execution of a perfect strike, the ball only knocks down four pins. You see ten pins explode into the air, but the ball itself makes direct contact with only four of them. A domino effect knocks down the other six pins. It doesn't take a lot of power to make those four pins fall over, but it does require an extremely well-placed shot to set up an effective chain reaction. Only proper technique results in accuracy that is consistent enough to produce strike after strike.

3. If bowling were a game of power, the sport would be dominated by former football players, body builders, and professional wrestlers. It isn't. Professional bowlers come in all shapes and sizes! Two of the best professional bowlers who ever appeared on TV were Earl "the Pearl" Anthony and Nelson Burton, Jr. They were not muscle-bound behemoths. They were two of the smoothest bowlers you ever saw, and two of the greatest who ever lived. Both made a good living by regularly beating power bowlers, because they relied on nearly flawless technique.

You get the idea. There is a place for power in the game of bowling, but it is *not* fundamental to the development of championship caliber skills. As in any sport, there are both *basic* and *advanced* skills. The *stance*, *pushaway*, *armswing*, and *release* are the basic skills. *Power* is one of the advanced skills. Build your game on a solid foundation of the *basics* because without them, you will *never* be able to develop advanced skills. Without them, nothing else matters (even if you're lucky).

About absolute truth number 2, what you do: The study of physics taught Lenny the principle of cause and effect. Applied to bowling, it means that where the ball goes and how it behaves depends entirely upon what *you* do to it. If you want your first shot to hit the pocket, then you need to develop techniques that enable you to send the ball into the pocket. It's really that simple.

Look at it this way. The approach is fifteen feet long. The lane, foul line to headpin, is sixty feet long. The length of the lane actually *amplifies* any error you make in your delivery by a factor of four! If you are one inch off at the foul line, the ball may end up as much as four inches off once it gets to the pins. This is why *what you do* must be repeatable, so that your results are *predictable*. It is why learning a proper technique is so important, so that you do the right things, not the wrong things (which get magnified). It prevents or, at the very least, reduces the variations in your delivery that destroy your scores and make you utter the inevitable curse, "These lanes *suck!*"

This principle holds the key not just to making you a better bowler but also to making you a better sportsman and person. How? By helping you learn to take responsibility for yourself. You see, it's easy to make excuses for failure, something for which bowlers are famous. This absolute truth forces you to face the reality that if your ball misses the target, it's because *you* made it miss the target. Once you can admit that you made a mistake, it becomes a simple matter to figure out what it was. You can then eliminate that mistake by making an *adjustment* to your delivery. Learning to adjust is what makes you better.

About absolute truth number 3, the ball travels a line: This statement is so simple and painfully obvious that you are probably wondering how it could possibly be of any importance to improving your game. To Lenny, it is the holy grail for which he spent decades searching.

What is good technique? This concept, the line, or more accurately the target line, provides the key to answering that all-important question. When combined with the other absolute truths, it unlocks the secret to determining what is important and what is not. It boils down to this: *Good technique is repeatable, puts the ball on your target line, and keeps it there.* Any advice that doesn't follow this rule is *garbage* because it leads to unreliable techniques.

This line begins at your shoulder the moment you take your stance and continues all the way down to the pins. It consists of two parts:

1. The path along which you carry the ball during your delivery
2. The path the ball follows once you release it

Good technique forms these two parts into one line seamlessly and effortlessly. Your improvement as a bowler (higher scores) relies on your:

- Learning to visualize this line in your stance. To do this, you must first roll a practice shot. The track the ball follows establishes a line. This line will be a function of the lane conditions. You need to visualize this line ending up in the pocket.
- Practicing the skills as described, so that you get the ball on that line and keep it there throughout your delivery.

TIP This line provides the basis for another advanced skill: reading lane conditions. Once your line is established, only two things can change it: variation in your technique or in lane conditions. Properly maintained lanes are mechanically cleaned and then dressed with oil every day. This creates the lane condition. Balls rolling on the lane move this oil around, changing that condition. If you eliminate deviations in your delivery, any change in your ball's trajectory must relate to the lane condition. Reading these changes becomes much easier as you gain confidence in the consistency of your skills.

Forty years of bowling taught Lenny that his father had been right—you need to build on a solid foundation. By themselves, the stance, pushaway, armswing, and release are just things you do to throw a ball down a lane to produce random results. These same four acts, developed into *skills* based upon three simple yet universal truths, became a *delivery system*. They became a series of finely tuned motions, knitted together, which enabled him to become one of the elite bowlers in every league in which he competed.

More important, these movements are so simple and well defined that he found he could teach them to anyone! There is only one thing Lenny likes more than bowling well: teaching other people how to bowl well. It takes him back to his first bowling experience. He had watched that other guy in awe and wondered *How does he do that?* Now he knows:

- The **S**tance puts the ball on a line to the target, allowing …
- the **P**ushaway to move the ball along that line and set up …
- the **A**rmswing, which develops ball speed along that line, allowing …
- the **RE**lease to smoothly send the ball onto the lane without altering its trajectory.

Are you beginning to understand how easy the game of bowling can be? Competency at any level depends on the mastery of only four basic skills. The real beauty of the **SPARE** system is not its simplicity, but that it works so well. Virtually anybody can learn and master it.

CHAPTER 3

The Stance

A proper stance is important because it aims your shot. It also sets up a consistent and effective delivery, ensures effortless transition to the next skill, and positions you to walk correctly, even though a very heavy weight is swinging from one side of your torso. Most important, the correct stance puts your ball *directly on the target line.* A bad stance does none of this.

Okay, let's get started. You have stepped up onto the approach, have picked your ball up from the return, and are standing on your normal starting spot.

Technique

1. Look down and note *exactly* where your feet are positioned.
2. Visualize the line your ball will travel, noting which arrow this line passes over.
3. Stand erect.
4. Face that arrow (it is your target).
5. Insert your fingers into the ball as tightly as possible, and then stretch your hand around the ball until the thumb slides easily into place.
6. Take a deep breath, *relax*, and *focus* on the following elements.
7. Shift all your weight to the foot that corresponds to the hand you're holding the ball with; use the other foot for balance only.

8. Dip your shoulder *straight down* as far as it will comfortably go. Do not force it down.
9. Anchor your elbow to your side.
10. Aim your forearm directly at your target.
11. Rotate your wrist to position your hand under the ball, but continue to support it with *both* hands.

TIP Of the four basic skills, the stance has the most elements. It may take a while for you to become comfortable with it. Practice it at home, in front of a mirror. It won't cost you a dime, and the results will be worth it. Training yourself at home will allow you to reduce the number of elements you need in your checklist once you hit the lanes.

Discussion

As you can see, the stance is composed of eleven elements. It is the most complicated of the basic skills. No kidding! The **SPARE** system is so easy that the most complicated thing you're going to have to learn is how to stand still properly. The following comments explain why every single one of these elements is vital.

1. *Position your feet.* For any of your skills to be useful, they must be repeatable. The lane's approach area is designed as it is for this very reason: to allow you to make the *precise* location of your stance repeatable.

   A bowling alley is 41–42 inches wide and consists of 39 boards side by side. The boards that make up the approach are lined up with the boards of the lane. Markers in the form of dots are built into the approach area so that you can easily note exactly which boards you have put your feet on. These dots line up with the arrows you will see about fifteen feet beyond the foul line. These arrows are the targets you will aim for, because they are closer than the pins.

The line your ball travels is determined by two points: your starting position and the arrow or other target that you aim for. Obviously, changing either of these points alters this line. Starting at a particular spot and then delivering your ball so that it rolls over a specific target will result in a strike. To repeat the process, you must continue to start at that exact spot and roll your ball over the same target.

TIP Changing where you stand is the most common adjustment bowlers need to make as lane conditions change. Keep things simple; alter your starting position while aiming for the same target on the lane. Moving your stance to the left brings the ball to the right side of the pins; moving it to the right brings the ball to the left side of the pins. This is how you zero in on the pocket—by moving the position of your stance one board at a time. This concept is also used for making spares.

TIP Since precision is so important to any skill, it is helpful to draw a line on the toe of the weight-bearing shoe. This line lets you quickly position your stance in exactly the same spot time after time. A dot will suffice, but a line also gives you a sense of direction.

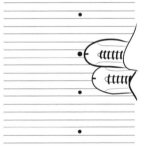

2. *Visualize your line.* This element establishes your target line. It is what practice shots (sometimes called shadow balls) are for, so that you can see how your ball will track once competition begins. Learning to visualize this line is a huge step forward for any bowler. It develops and strengthens your mental game. It takes your mind off distractions and puts your focus where

it belongs: on your technique. This element becomes easier with practice.

3. *Stand erect.* An upright stance allows you to be smooth and relaxed at the beginning of your approach. It also helps prevent "rushing the foul line."

   The sports of track and field and scuba diving teach that the feet follow the head. To run faster, lean forward. To dive, point your head down. In bowling, crouching over in your stance leads to the head getting in front of the feet. The feet will naturally try to catch up and cause you to rush the shot. When this happens, you will feel that your timing is off. This is a common symptom of being tired and is easily cured by standing up straighter in your stance.

4. *Face the target.* This element is invaluable, because it aims *you.* It determines the *proper direction* of your delivery. Squaring *your shoulders* to the target every time squares *you* to your target every time. This component of the stance helps ensure consistent accuracy.

5. *Grip the ball.* You cannot deliver consistent shots without a secure grip on the ball. Nothing will destroy your concentration faster than feeling the ball start to slip off your hand prematurely. Two things determine the security of your grip: fit and friction.

   Good fit comes from having a ball custom drilled specifically for you by people who know what they're doing. Have this done by a qualified professional, ideally at the bowling center at which you compete. Please note: a ball that fits poorly may cause blisters. These can quickly rupture, begin to bleed, and lead to an infection. You do not want that.

   Friction is a different matter altogether. Keep your hands dry by judicious use of a cotton towel, and always have a rosin bag handy. (Blowing gently into the thumbhole can help too!)

In addition to controlling fit and friction, you have to develop a consistent routine when you are up on the approach. You must learn to put your hand into the ball the same way each and every time. This helps to ensure that the hand comes out of the ball the same way each and every time. This is an example of how a good stance complements the other skills. The grip created here enhances the certainty of a reliable release later.

Start by placing your fingers into the ball as deeply and as tightly as possible. Why? Again, it's about being consistent. Tight fingers = consistent release; loose fingers = inconsistent release. Simple! The next step is to stretch your hand around the ball until the thumb can easily be inserted into the thumb-hole. If necessary, test your grip by hanging the ball at your side and swinging it back and forth a few times to make sure it doesn't slip. If it does, dry your hand with a towel, apply some rosin, and start over.

TIP *Never* leave your thumb inside the ball while waiting for someone else to bowl. It quickly begins to perspire. Excessive moisture acts as a lubricant and *will* compromise your grip.

6. *Take a deep breath.* You have completed the preliminaries of your stance. You are positioned. Now you must set up your delivery. Taking a deep breath at this point relaxes your body. Tension causes bad shots by making you "choke." With tension gone and nerves under control, it is easier to focus on what you need to do next. One deep breath—it may seem unimportant, but it makes a big difference.
7. *Put your weight on one foot* (the right foot for right-handed bowlers; the left foot for left-handed bowlers). This

element of your stance is a consistency insurance policy. It guarantees that you will always take your first step with the same foot. Try it. Put all your weight on one foot, lean forward, and see which foot moves first automatically, without your thinking about it. This is critical when your concentration is blown because you need one more strike for your first 300 game. It is one less thing you have to worry about.

This *one-footed* stance also helps you to walk straighter during your delivery, making certain that the ball stays on its line. Here's how. If your weight is distributed on both feet, your first step requires that you shift part of your weight sideways to one foot or the other. Sideways movement is off-line movement. Remember, the efficient and effective delivery *gets the ball on the line and keeps it there* (Recall absolute truth number 3: The ball travels a line toward the pins.).

NOTE This one-footed stance creates a three- or five-step approach. If you use a four-step approach and prefer not to modify your technique, ignore this element. Instead, concentrate on keeping your feet close together. If you are just taking up this sport, I highly recommend developing a five-step approach, because it produces superior results.

8. *Dip your shoulder comfortably.* This may be the most crucial part of the stance. Here is a list of the benefits created by this one simple element, all of which will happen automatically.

   • It clears the path for your armswing. While standing erect, dipping your shoulder *straight down* causes your head to move to that side, while keeping you square with your target line. Your head weighs about ten pounds, so to maintain balance, your hips move in the opposite direction. With your hips out of the way, your arm is now able to swing more like a pendulum. The consistency with which you perform this dip is critical to the pendulum motion. Doing it to a degree of comfort makes it repeatable.

- The movement of your head to the side places one eye more directly above the target line. For most people, this will be your dominant eye. This enhances the accuracy of your pushaway by giving you a more direct line of sight down the target line. It's just like aiming a rifle.

- Dipping the shoulder enhances your ability to walk the ball in a straight line. Look at your footprints in the snow or in the sand. You will see that as you move forward, your footprints move from side to side. This is because as you walk, your weight shifts from side to side. If you are shifting side to side, so is the ball. Remember, we want to get the ball on a line and keep it there. Any sideward movement is taboo. Dropping your shoulder changes your sense of equilibrium. You begin placing one foot more directly in front of the other, as if you are walking a tightrope. You will move straight forward, the ball will move straight forward, and you will have one more reason to visit the beach: to study your footprints in the sand. Life is good.

- Dipping your shoulder also enhances the consistency of your delivery by allowing your head to remain steady throughout your approach. Swinging any heavy object from one shoulder naturally pulls that shoulder down. Allowing this to happen during your approach means that your head changes position during your approach. Keeping your head steady is crucial to your ability to concentrate. For this reason alone, it is worth embracing what

nature wants and *dip that shoulder* before taking the
first step.

9. *Anchor your elbow.* Champion archers bring consisten-
    cy to their shots by drawing the bowstring back and
    anchoring their hand to the exact same spot on their
    chin every single time. This principle works for bowl-
    ing as well. Keeping your elbow anchored tight to your
    side stabilizes your arm and provides a consistent
    starting point for your shot.
10. *Aim your forearm.* Absolute truth number 3: The ball
    travels a line toward the pins. Pointing your forearm
    directly at your target puts the ball on that line. Having
    the forearm pointing *along* that line ensures that it *stays
    there* once you begin your approach. Previous elements
    of the stance have aimed *you*; this one aims *the ball.*
11. *Keep your hand under the ball.* This element is a minor
    one but is important because it sets up your arm to
    swing like a pendulum, keeping the ball on its intend-
    ed target line. Remember to continue to support the
    ball with both hands. You are now fully prepared to
    initiate your approach.

P.S. No mention is made of *how high* to hold the ball in the
stance. This is a matter of personal strength and comfort.
Ball height during your stance is important because gravity
will be used to produce the speed of your shot, not muscle
power. I discuss this as part of your next skill, the pushaway.

TIP Once you are in your stance, run through a mental
checklist to ensure a uniform posture from frame to frame.
This not only promotes the consistency of the remainder of
your actual delivery but it also engages your mind to take
control at this point. The most important elements of this
checklist are weight on one foot, shoulder dipped, forearm
aimed at the target, and hand under the ball.

An effective stance

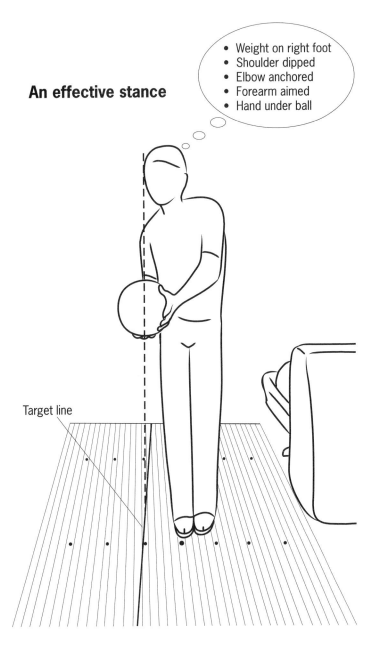

- Weight on right foot
- Shoulder dipped
- Elbow anchored
- Forearm aimed
- Hand under ball

Target line

CHAPTER 4

The Pushaway

The pushaway is important because it determines the speed and direction of your shot. This skill puts you in charge of the ball. Developing and using a good, solid pushaway gives you a distinct advantage over any bowler who chooses to ignore this skill.

Technique

Keeping your hand positioned *under* the ball, push it directly toward its target with *both* hands until your arm is completely straight.

TIP Like the stance, this skill can be practiced at home. A mirror isn't even necessary, just a target. The act of pushing the ball away until your arm is straight must become a habit.

Discussion

Yes, that's really all there is to performing the pushaway. It is by far the simplest and easiest skill to master, yet it is the most underutilized. There are a few things you need to know about this skill in order to understand both its importance and how to use it effectively.

- For the sake of your timing, if you use a three-step delivery, the pushaway should begin before you take the first step. If you use a four-step delivery, it should begin simultaneously with the first step. If you use a five-step delivery, it should begin with the second step.

- The pushaway should be smooth and deliberate but not aggressive. An aggressive pushaway can pull you forward, loosen your grip on the ball, and throw you off-balance. This will affect how you walk and may ruin the consistency of the remainder of your approach.
- The direction of the pushaway can be straight out toward your target, or it can be straight out and down toward your target line. It should not go upward or straight down. It must never go sideways.
- The pushaway sets up the armswing. For this reason, you *must* focus on maintaining a wrist position that keeps your hand *under* the ball. This is critical. It allows the ball to drop straight down at the beginning of the armswing, keeping it on the target line.
- The *height* of the ball at the end of your pushaway determines the *speed* of your shot. The higher the ball is at the end of the pushaway, the faster it will swing and the harder it will be to hang on to. Keep this in mind as you develop this skill.

Remember, the ball should never be in charge of its own delivery. This skill puts *you* in charge of the shot, so pay attention to it.

TIP The pushaway is one of the adjustments you can make to your delivery. Since you will be using gravity to produce the speed of the shot (a concept to be covered in the following chapter), you can produce more or less speed by altering the height to which you push the ball.

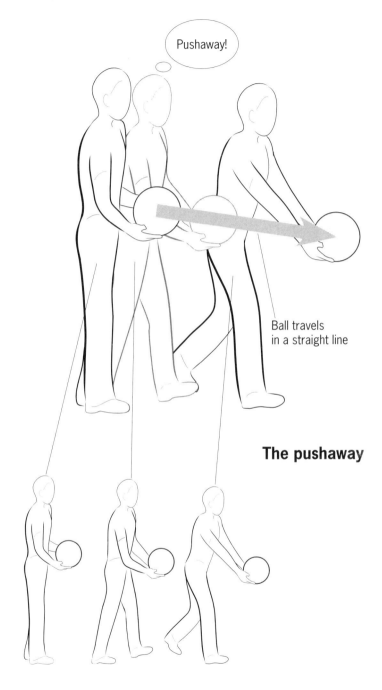

The pushaway

CHAPTER 5

The Armswing

No skill is more important than the *armswing*. It develops ball speed and ensures that the ball stays directed along the target line. It develops your timing. It enables a smooth release. It even plays a role in determining how much your ball will hook after it is released.

Performed properly, your armswing is a tremendous asset. Screw it up, and it becomes your worst nightmare. Inconsistent armswings cause more bad shots than all of the other skills combined.

Technique

1. *The downswing.* Immediately at the end of your push-away, allow the ball to just *drop*. The other arm will automatically swing away to maintain your balance. Focus on keeping your arm straight and your wrist rotated to position your hand directly under and then behind the ball.
2. *The backswing.* As soon as your arm is vertical, apply the brakes to gently bring the backswing to a halt before it can twist your shoulders out of alignment with the target. Focus on keeping your hand directly behind the ball.
3. *The forward swing.* As the direction of your armswing changes, shift your mental focus from your wrist position to your release point. Do not power the ball forward.

4. *The follow-through*. Don't worry about the follow-through. Deliver the ball correctly and the follow-through will happen automatically. It is an indicator of your success, nothing more.

TIP During the execution of the armswing, forget about the ball. It is only along for the ride.

TIP During the execution of your armswing, only three points require your attention:

1. The *drop point*, which occurs at the very end of the pushaway
2. The *stop point*, which is the end of the backswing
3. The *release point*

Physically, the armswing is complicated; the mental portion must not be. Keep it simple by thinking, *Drop, stop, and roll.* By focusing on these three points and hitting them consistently, you ensure repeatable, accurate shots.

Discussion

The armswing is what separates great bowlers from everyone else. It is the most challenging skill to master for a number of reasons:

- It's a sneaky little devil. You can't see it. It drops out of sight at the end of your pushaway and then stays out of sight until *after* you have delivered the ball. This skill is a *mental* exercise.
- The armswing mechanics are more complicated than those of any other skill.
- It must coordinate with your walk.
- It has four distinct parts: the downswing, the backswing, the forward swing, and the follow-through. Mentally you must deal with each one separately.

The secret to taming this skill lies in the KISS principle, the engineering adage to "Keep it simple, stupid." Any
engineer will tell you that the simpler something is, the more
reliable it will be.

When considering the development of your armswing,
it is helpful to think of the motion of a pendulum. This is just
a ball hanging from a string, swinging back and forth, trac-
ing the same path, over and over. It's exactly what you want
to accomplish: an arm that swings your ball along its target
line over and over.

That concept is simple enough, but your ball is *not*
swinging from a string. Your mechanism is infinitely more
complex. There are hundreds of moving parts involved:
muscles, ligaments, tendons, bones, and joints. You may ask,
"How do I make my hand, wrist, arm, and shoulder act like
a simple string?" Find one thing that makes everything else
behave like a simple string. That one thing is the *position of
your wrist*. The wrist defines the alignment of everything else
in your armswing mechanics. It also determines how they
will interact with each other. All you need to do is find the
one wrist position that makes your arm swing the ball in the
direction of its target.

Here are three tips to help you develop an effective
and consistent armswing, one that generates adequate power while keeping the ball on the target line:

Tip 1 *Focus on maintaining your wrist position.* Your wrist is
the most important anatomical structure in your armswing.
It moves side to side, it flexes, and it rotates. A good wrist
brace will control variations in the side-to-side and flexing
movements. This lets you mentally focus on its rotation,
which, in turn, affects the direction of your armswing.

An approach lasts a mere two to three seconds. That's
enough time to focus on only one thing, and that must be the
rotation of your wrist. This creates the consistency required

for pinpoint accuracy over and over again. Remember, control your wrist and you control the whole armswing.

NOTE The rotation of your wrist is described by the position it creates for your thumb in relation to the face of a clock. If your wrist is positioned so that your hand is under (or behind) the ball, this is the twelve o'clock position. The thumb is pointing straight up like the hour hand of a clock indicating the noon hour. If your wrist places the hand directly on the side of the ball, this is called the nine o'clock position (for a right-hander). Your thumb would be pointing at the number 9 on a clock face. This influences both armswing technique and ball hook, consequences to be discussed later.

Tip 2 *Keep the armswing compact.* Based on your individual anatomy, your armswing has physical limitations built into it. The farther you try to go beyond those limits, the more inconsistent your swing becomes. A compact armswing avoids those limitations.

Tip 3 *Leave your ego at home; it will work against you.* As with any sport, bowling has its moments of frustration and embarrassment. Those moments are no reason for you to lose your composure. Teammates are relying on you to perform and set a good example. Remember, your armswing is a mental exercise. Calm, rational thinking is required, and ego will not provide that. Instead, it will demand that you punish those uncooperative pins by exaggerating the power of your armswing in order to teach them a lesson. This rarely produces a result which improves your self-esteem or your score.

Now let's take a look at the individual elements that make up a productive armswing.

1. *The downswing:* In your stance, you rotated the wrist so that your hand was *under* the ball (or as close to this

as your individual anatomy would comfortably allow). During the pushaway, you maintained this wrist position. Why? So that during the downswing, your arm, unaided by muscle power, could drop straight down and imitate a pendulum. This action takes advantage of gravity to accelerate the ball. Since nothing is more reliable than this natural law, use it to achieve consistent ball speed rather than tiring the muscles in your arm.

Another reason the 12 o'clock wrist position is important is that it keeps the ball from striking *you*. A 9 o'clock wrist position (3 o'clock for a lefty), coupled with a true pendulum swing may result in the ball brushing against your thigh on the way back and glancing off your ankle as it moves forward. The first is distracting; the second hurts (a lot). By themselves, either of these scenarios will force your ball off that all-important target line. More important, it destroys both your concentration and your confidence.

NOTE Bouncing a bowling ball off your ankle even once will make for a very long night. To avoid this, you will compensate by swinging your arm out and away from your body. Since the ball is going along for a ride, it will follow the same path, which is an arc. Only one point on that arc is in the direction of your target. Consistency will be impossible.

By concentrating on keeping your wrist rotated to the twelve o'clock position, you minimize the chance of the ball making contact with you during *any* part of the armswing. This simple act has other significant benefits:

- It focuses your mind on *technique*, allowing you to ignore other distractions (like Mark).
- It actually *causes* your arm to swing straight along the target line. This brings consistency to the

direction of your shot and enables you to focus on the next element, the backswing.

- It keeps energy loaded into your shot. Up to this point, the use of muscle power has been kept to an absolute minimum. Here is where it begins to come into play. The natural position for your hand is facing the side of your body—the nine o'clock position for righties, the three o'clock for lefties. It requires the use of muscles to force the wrist clockwise or counterclockwise, which was done in the stance. Any rotation maintained in your wrist here will be reversed later. When you release the ball, your hand will be rotating in the opposite direction, causing the ball to hook. Performing this task to a set position makes it consistent, reliable, and predictable. Best of all, this will happen automatically.

Another important facet of your approach happens automatically at this point. The momentum of the ball, created by the downswing, causes you to lean forward. This is a natural consequence of human anatomy interacting with the laws of physics. This is where your forward lean *should* happen because it will have a minimal effect on the speed of your walk. Remember, you do not want to rush to the foul line. Leaning forward tends to increase the pace of the feet, but the ball swinging backward slows you down. These two actions counteracting each other give you one less thing to think about.

2. *The backswing:* If the armswing is the hardest skill to master, the backswing is the hardest element of this skill to master. This crucial element will destroy your entire delivery. How? By twisting your posture out of alignment.

The techniques you have learned so far have gotten the ball on a line and enabled you to keep it there. So far, so good. In the backswing, however, you are moving in one direction but the ball is moving in the opposite direction. The laws of physics dictate that some force is required in order to change the direction of the ball. This force will tend to twist your torso. If this happens, your shoulders will no longer be square to your target and your armswing will no longer be on its target line.

There are two ways to deal with this, and you must pick one of them:

- *One way:* Compensate for the twist by visualizing a sheet of glass that runs along your target line. Maintain your armswing within that glass. This thought process is used by golfers to aid in developing the swing of their club. The advantage of this technique is that it permits the development of a *power swing*, one that goes very high during the backswing. The disadvantage is that it tests the physical limits of your anatomy, which, as previously discussed, leads to inconsistency.
- *A better way:* Prevent the twisting altogether by *controlling* the backswing. You will sacrifice *some* power for the sake of accuracy, but remember, bowling is a game of skill, not power. Any accuracy you can gain is an advantage, especially when you consider how little power you have to give up in order to achieve it.

The secret to preventing shoulder twist is to determine the natural upper limit of your backswing and then never allow it to go beyond that point. To do this, stand erect with both arms hanging straight down at your side and the palms of both hands facing forward. Simultaneously, move both arms *straight back* as far as they will comfortably go. This simple exercise defines the upper limit of your backswing: Your swing arm is as far back as it will go, and your shoulders are still square with your target. Just to satisfy your own curiosity, drop your other arm down and see how much higher you can make the swing arm go—probably quite a bit.

Notice that in order to achieve the higher backswing, you have rotated your wrist out of position, turned your shoulders, or bent at the waist. Any of these can cause the types of inconsistencies that destroy scoring ability but are synonymous with the power swing.

The controlled backswing can also develop considerable power but does so in a very different way. When you apply the brakes, muscles, tendons, and ligaments are used. Because the hand is rigidly positioned behind the ball at this stage and your shoulders are being kept square to your target, these structures absorb all the energy created during the downswing. They return that energy to the ball during the forward swing. How? Good question.

To bring the backswing to a halt, force is exerted by your muscles. This force continues to be applied even after the ball has stopped, but it now accelerates the ball toward its target. This is extremely reliable because it happens automatically, generating power yet maintaining the consistent accuracy of your shots. To keep your shoulders square, it is imperative that you *do not* apply additional muscle power at this point.

Whichever backswing you select, the importance of maintaining the rotation of your wrist remains the same as in the downswing. Since I'm trying to teach you the best techniques possible, for the rest of this chapter I am assuming you have chosen the *better* technique, the controlled backswing.

3. *The forward swing:* By controlling the backswing and maintaining your wrist position, you've set the stage for the forward swing. You must still ignore your

natural instincts to apply additional power to your shot. The ball is still behind you and the *conscious* application of additional power, at this point, will pull your shoulders out of alignment. This will cause your shot to go off-line.

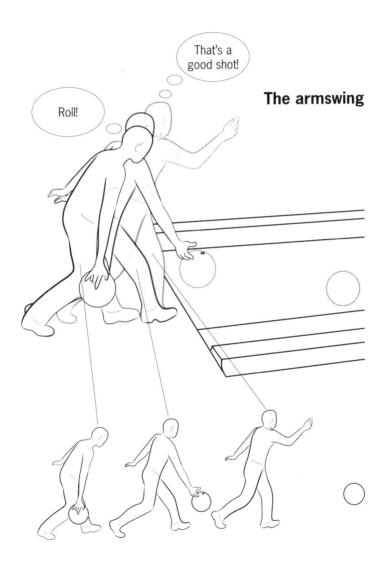

The armswing

At the beginning of the forward swing, shift your focus from the *wrist* to your *release point*. This strategy removes the control you exert over the muscle groups governing the wrist position and shifts it to the muscle groups that will rule the fingers as they lift the ball out onto the lane. This allows the following good things to happen automatically:

- Energy was stored in your armswing to stop the backswing. That energy is now released, accelerating the ball naturally and automatically along the target line.
- Because the controlled swing keeps the backswing lower than a power swing, the ball is much more likely to arrive at the foul line at the exact same moment as your sliding foot. This is perfect timing.
- Focusing on the release point keeps the shot on the target line.
- Focusing on the release point allows the wrist to begin to unscrew itself; it rotates back in the direction of its natural position. This reversal of the wrist's rotation continues throughout the remainder of the armswing, placing the fingers on the side of the ball during the release. In this position, they impart rotation to the ball, causing it to hook.

4. *The follow-through:* This occurs *after* the ball has been released. As a part of the armswing skill, it is unimportant. It is something which happens properly if you have delivered the ball properly; nothing more. It is, however, an important indicator.

- If the follow-through lines up with your target, you made a good shot.

- If it ends to the right of your target, your wrist was rotated too far clockwise during the backswing. This is true no matter which hand you use. If you are right-handed, this causes your backswing to go behind your back, which makes your forward swing go out to the right. For left-handers, this causes the backswing to go out and away from your body, which means the forward swing will head to the right.
- If the follow-through ends up to the left of your target, your wrist was rotated too far counterclockwise during the backswing. For right-handers, this causes the backswing to go out and away from the body, which makes the forward swing go to the left. For lefties, this problem causes the backswing to go behind your back, which means the forward swing will move out to the left.

In any case, the follow-through indicates how well you have made your armswing behave when you couldn't see it. Don't practice the follow-through. Practice paying attention to what it's telling you. A lot of things happen during the armswing. By performing the elements of this skill as described, most of those things will happen automatically. They will be consistent, reliable, and predictable. More important, this skill will help you to strengthen your mental game, which will produce better results in the form of higher scores for you.

TIP Like the stance and pushaway, the armswing is a skill that can be practiced at home, in front of a mirror. Pay close attention to what happens to the *direction* of your armswing with various wrist positions.

Practice at home

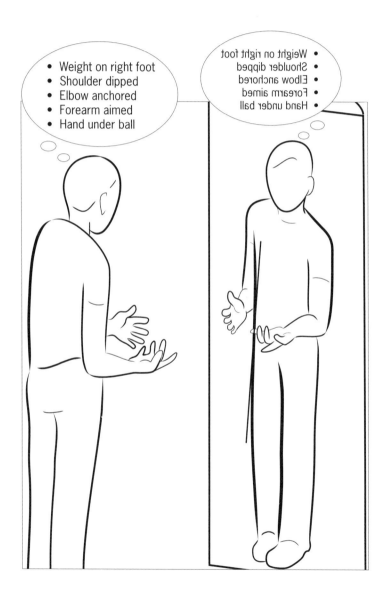

CHAPTER 6

The Release

The importance of the *release* is obvious; it launches your shot down the lane. Not so obvious, but equally important, is *what your release tells you.* If the ball comes off your hand smoothly, it is saying that you performed the prior skills properly, that your wrist was well positioned, that your timing was good, and that you have made a good shot. If the release goes poorly, it is telling you that you made a mistake at some point in your delivery.

This is the skill that gives your game that personal touch—literally. Muscle power is allowed here, because it can be applied beneficially, without too much concern for inconsistency.

Now it's time to learn how to take your best shot.

Technique

1. *Initiate the release.* Your arm is swinging forward. The *instant* it reaches vertical, relax your grip on the ball by removing the pressure your thumb is exerting on it. Concentrate on feeling the weight of the ball shift onto your fingers.
2. *Apply lift.* With the thumb now free of the ball, maintain the rigid posture of your wrist as much as possible. Focus on accelerating your *hand* along the target line, using the strength of your fingers to loft the ball out onto the lane (lift and loft are synonymous).

TIP Like the other skills, a consistent release happens in your mind first. The ball should not be allowed to simply pull itself free of your grip. Flip a coin like a referee at a football game. Notice that the thumb moves and the fingers don't. This action is identical to how a bowling ball is released. To ensure a consistent and reliable release, mentally picture yourself flipping a coin out onto the lanes.

TIP Wearing a wrist support is *highly* recommended. It will help prevent the wrist from flexing during the release. This keeps the fingers in the ball longer, allowing them to impart more rotation to the ball. It also allows you to feel what your wrist is doing during the armswing (when you can't see it). Finally, note that tremendous forces affect the wrist during the entire delivery. Wrist supports greatly reduce the severity of repetitive stress injuries that bowlers are prone to suffer.

TIP After the ball has left your hand, pose at the foul line until the ball has passed over its target. This ensures the consistency of your whole delivery. It also allows you to study the line the ball travels and look for changing lane conditions. If you can't maintain your balance, you have delivered the ball too aggressively. You will be inconsistent, and unable to observe or adjust to changes in the lane conditions.

Discussion

Let's take a quick look at the two elements that make up a consistent release so that you will understand how to perform and adjust this final skill.

1. *Initiating the release:* The release terminates the forward portion of the armswing. It happens in the blink of an eye, so you don't have the luxury of time to think about it, unless as instructed, you have been focused

on this *exact* instant since the end of the backswing. This point is actually determined for you when your arm is straight up and down, because that is when the ball is exerting its greatest force against your grip.

Take advantage of the laws of physics by just going along with what nature is telling you to do anyway; let the ball roll off your thumb. When the thumb releases its pressure, you feel the weight of the ball shift onto your fingers. This happens both quickly and automatically. It is called the explosion point because it is where you may apply your strength to *explode* out of the ball.

2. *Loft the ball:* If you choose to apply power, now is the time, because only the muscles in your fingers will be involved and they aren't powerful enough to significantly alter the path of your shot. They are, however, extremely consistent. Employing them at this point provides your ball with additional rotation. This makes the ball hook more and mix the pins up more effectively when it strikes them.

TIP For the sake of your consistency, think *all or nothing* when deciding whether to apply power as you loft the ball onto the lane. Anything else promotes variations in the ball's path.

While simply letting go of the ball may sound like the easiest thing in the world, it is not. It must be done with such precise consistency and relies on so many other conditions that it is a challenging skill to perfect. These conditions include:

- The fit of your equipment
- Timing
- Your grip
- The execution of the previous skills
- Your wrist position

The release

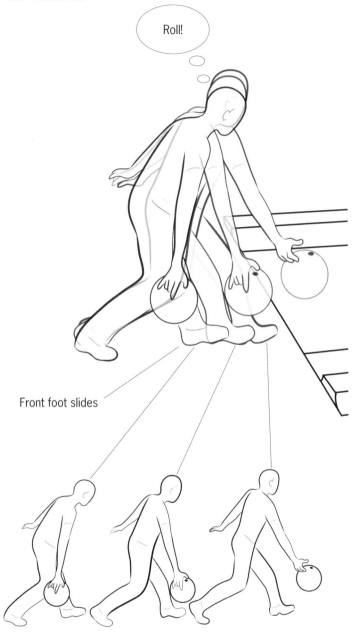

Front foot slides

All these physical elements must come together perfectly for a smooth release that produces a consistent and devastating shot. Practicing the skills as described and purchasing quality equipment help ensure that happens. However, there is one more element to consider in the development of your release. It is intangible but may be the most important part of your game. It is your confidence.

This is the mental element that is the secret to ensuring that your release is successful over and over again. Lack of confidence is what makes you believe that you must steer the ball. It prevents you from trusting yourself and giving up control of the ball, hanging on to it beyond that explosion point. This leads to shots that are pulled off the target line, which leads to bad scores, which causes a lack of confidence, which leads to more poor shots, which leads to … well, you get the idea. It's a vicious cycle.

Learning and practicing good technique breaks that cycle. It is much easier to unleash your shot when you know, without a doubt, that your stance, pushaway, and armswing have your ball on the target line. Understand that the techniques you have mastered will make the ball roll over its target again and again. Rest assured that it will hit the pins with more than enough power to make mincemeat of them. Once you do, you will look forward to the release because you will enjoy watching the show. That's what confidence is all about.

The release is the worst possible moment for something to go wrong. Practice your skills, trust yourself, turn that ball loose with confidence, and enjoy the successes you will have earned.

CHAPTER 7

Making Spares

The secret of a 200 average is to become proficient at making spares. To put the importance of spare making into perspective, consider this: The highest possible score in a game with *no* spares (or strikes) is 90. The highest possible score in an all-spare game is 190. Knocking down just 10 more pins makes a difference of 100 pins in the final score. Shoot just two or three strikes in a row and Bam! You have a 200 game.

Making spares is easy once you have zeroed in on the pocket. *Spot bowling* (using the arrows on the lane as your targets) is the key. This aiming system operates on the theory that a target 15 feet away is easier to hit than a target 60 feet away. Once you have established where to stand and which target to hit in order to put the ball in the pocket, follow this rule of thumb:

Right-handers: For every pin to the right of the pocket, move your stance three boards to the left. For every pin to the left of the pocket, move your stance four boards to the right. Do not change your target.

Left-handers: For every pin to the left of the pocket, move your stance three boards to the right. For every pin to the right of the pocket, move your stance four boards to the left. Do not change your target.

This generalization can be applied to combination spares as well as single-pin spares. The trick is to think of combinations of pins as single-pin spares. For example, to make a 5–7 split, a right-hander should aim for the nine pin. A ball heading for the nine pin (which isn't even there) is very likely to graze the five pin and send it toward the seven pin. Get the idea?

The exception to the rule is the ten pin for right-handers and the seven pin for left-handers. There is much less room for error when shooting these spares because they bring the gutters into play. Avoiding the gutter is paramount because once the ball enters one, it is out of play. If it jumps back out, any pins it knocks down do not count. To avoid the gutter, consider the following:

- To make the ten pin spare, a righty should move the stance as far to the left as possible and use the area around the middle arrow as the target. This keeps the target line away from the ditch longer. It also causes the ball to hook less because there is always more lane conditioning oil in the middle of the lane.
- To make the seven pin spare, a lefty should move the stance as far to the right as possible and use the area between the third and fourth arrows as a target (left-handers tend to have more natural hook to their shots).

TIP Two common combinations are almost impossible to make. These are the 4–6 and the 7–10 splits. When faced with them, make sure that you knock down one of the pins. Do not try to make the spare. The precision necessary is beyond human capabilities. Getting one pin has three positive consequences:

1. A pin hit by a ball will give you a chance of actually making the spare by bouncing around a bit. This is where luck becomes important. A missed pin will just stand there until it is removed by the sweep, costing you and your team pin count.

2. Games are won and lost
   by that one pin. You
   want to be the bowler
   that wins by a single pin.
   (Encourage your oppo-
   nents to try to make these
   spares).
3. Staying calm and continu-
   ing to perform establishes
   you as a bowler, not a
   hothead.

Spot bowling

- Moving stance to the left
  moves ball's path to the right
- Moving stance to the right
  moves ball's path to the left
- The combination of repeatable
  skills and this targeting system
  will result in the precise accuracy
  required for you to become an elite
  bowler.

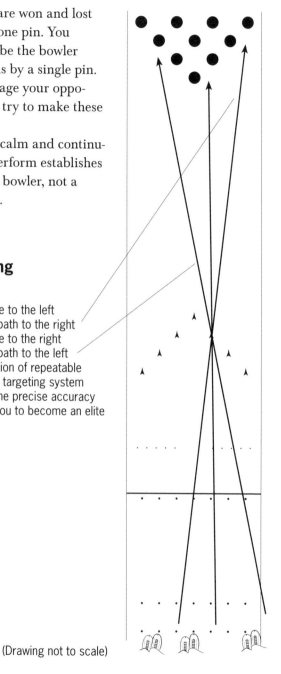

(Drawing not to scale)

CHAPTER 8

Making Basic Adjustments

Once you master the techniques described in the preceding chapters, you need to be able to apply them to varying lane conditions. Conditioning lanes is an art. Reading those conditions is an advanced skill, beyond the scope of this book. But I do want to touch briefly on this subject, to give you the broad outline.

Bowling in a league means competing on nearly identical conditions week after week. You will become comfortable applying your skills to playing a particular line because it produces the results you expect from yourself. That's human nature and it's a good thing. It means that whenever you go to *any* bowling alley, you have a starting point. You have a place to stand, a target to aim for, and a result to expect. You have established what can be called your standard shot, and that's important. It allows you to read the lanes.

At some point—it could be the next game on your home alleys or at a tournament somewhere else—you will deliver your standard shot, and the ball will not react as predicted. These are the times when your ability to be consistent is so important. Because you know your shot is consistent, only lane conditions make your ball misbehave. Figuring out what your ball is telling you about the lane condition is not difficult. There are only three basic messages it can send you:

1. If the ball doesn't make it to the pocket, it's telling you that there is more oil on the lanes than you are used to.

This is a common occurrence on freshly conditioned lanes. Possible adjustments include:

- Right-handers, move your stance to the right. Left-handers, move to the left.
- Slow the ball down by using a lower end point to your pushaway. This allows more time for your ball to hook.
- Set the ball down on the lane sooner. Less loft means the ball is in contact with the lane for a longer period of time. This allows the hooking action to carry it farther up into the pocket.

2. If the ball hits the pocket, it's telling you that the conditions are well suited to your skills. No adjustment is necessary.
3. If the ball goes up on the head pin or crosses over to the Brooklyn side, the ball is saying that there is less oil on the lanes than you are used to. This is a common condition on alleys late in the day, especially those that have seen a lot of use. To adjust:

- Right-handers, move your stance to the left. Left-handers, move to the right. For every two boards that you move your stance, move your target one board in the same direction. You want to get your ball onto the oil so your shots don't go out of control.
- Play an inside line. The most used line on any bowling alley is the second arrow, because this is the most effective shot for the average bowler. Any ball played between the second arrow and the gutter is referred to as an *outside* line. Any ball played between the second arrow and the middle of the

alley is referred to as an *inside* line. Whenever the ball hooks too much because the lanes are too dry, always move inside. That's where the oil will be.

- Increase the speed of your shot by raising the height of your pushaway. This causes the ball to slide farther down the lane, resulting in less hook at the back end.
- Loft the ball farther out onto the lane by standing up straighter during your delivery. Using less of the lane decreases the hook of the ball.
- Rotate your wrist clockwise (counterclockwise for left-handers) at the explosion point to reduce the hook of the ball. This is an advanced technique, but if you've made it this far, you are certainly entitled to try it.

There you have it—basic but standard adjustments every bowler should be able to make once they have achieved consistency. There are a few things to keep in mind to make adjustments effectively:

- Two lanes are rarely identical. When you are on a pair of lanes, as in most league play, pay attention to how the ball acts on *each* lane. Many bowlers don't realize this and are unable to string strikes together because they habitually play both lanes exactly the same. If one lane is giving you grief, adjust to that one and only that one.
- Lane conditions change gradually, but they do change. Remember, if you are competing on a team with five people, a nearly complete game is rolled on each lane before you bowl on it again.
- Three bad shots in a row tell you it is time to adjust.
- Make your adjustments small ones.
- Never adjust more than one skill at a time.

- Don't make any adjustments until your hand is stretched out and your muscles are loosened up. You can't accurately read the lanes until you can successfully deliver your standard shot, so take full advantage of shadow ball time.

CHAPTER 9

Random Thoughts and Tips

Here are some tips gleaned from over three decades of coaching bowlers. I hope they will add to your knowledge, enjoyment, and safety as you seek to improve your game.

🎳 While developing your game, set realistic goals. Of course, these depend on the skill level where you begin. Here are some examples starting as a novice:

- Bowl a complete game with no gutter balls.
- Bowl a complete game without a five-count (or less) on the first ball.
- Bowl a complete game without a six-count (or less) on the first ball.
- Bowl a 200 game.
- Bowl a complete game without an open frame.
- Bowl a complete game without missing the pocket on the first ball.
- Bowl a 600 series.
- Carry a 200 average for a season.
- Bowl a 700 series.
- Bowl a 300 game.
- Bowl an 800 series.

The skills you have learned from this book will enable you to accomplish *all* of these goals.

🎳 Everyone's anatomy is unique, so everybody's delivery will be unique. Perform the skills described in this text to the best of your ability, but remember to stay within your comfort zone. If you're comfortable with what you do, you'll be consistent at it.

🎳 Never keep score when practicing. Practice scores are absolutely meaningless and prevent you from focusing on training yourself to perform the skills necessary to produce higher scores.

🎳 When competing, ignore the scores until the game is over. It's hard to do, but allowing yourself to be distracted by paying attention to who's winning and who's losing keeps you from focusing on what you need to do to win.

🎳 Whether practicing or actually competing, endeavor to learn at least one thing every time you bowl. Don't be afraid to experiment with your technique. That's how to find out what works best for you.

🎳 If something in your technique causes you pain or discomfort of any kind, you are doing it wrong. Change your technique or seek advice from a qualified instructor.

🎳 During the summer months, cross-train by pitching horseshoes. Armswing and wrist position are key to success at this sport as well. Oh yeah, it's fun too.

🎳 When rolling shadow balls, ignore the pins left behind by the bowler in front of you. Deliver a pocket shot on each lane and then try for a ten pin and then a seven pin (especially if there isn't one there). This will confuse your opponents. Meanwhile, you are getting comfortable with these shots, while figuring out the lane conditions at the same time.

Whatever you do happens inside your head first. Practicing in front of a mirror develops a strong mental imagery of you doing the right things. Until you have developed your skills adequately, avoid watching people bowl badly. Their bad habits are easy to pick up.

"When you're not practicing, someone else is. When you meet that person, he's going to beat you."—author unknown

Except for the effect the stance has on it, your walk to the foul line is not addressed in this book. Your natural stride is just fine. It is comfortable and automatic. Your leg muscles are among the strongest in your body so they behave consistently all by themselves. Adjusting your walk is a *highly* advanced skill, so if it ain't broke, don't fix it.

At the end of your delivery, your slide should end up within six inches of the foul line. Adjust your stance until it does.

Besides a ball and shoes, a well-equipped bag will contain the following:

- A cotton towel to keep your hands dry.
- A microfiber towel to remove oil and dirt from your ball.
- A rosin bag to maintain a secure grip.
- A small bottle of baby powder. Applied to the back of the thumb it prevents sticking. Never apply it

to the front of the thumb, as it will cause you to lose your grip. Never put this stuff on the floor. Someone will step on it. They will slip and may fall and injure themselves.

- A wrist support to prevent wrist injuries and enhance ball control.
- Various grades of sandpaper to enlarge and smooth the ball's thumbhole.
- Ball cleaning solution to clean your ball at the end of the day's competition. A reactive resin ball absorbs oil like a sponge. Clean it with solvent both before and after bowling. This will maintain its performance and extend the life of the ball.

You may develop calluses on your fingers or thumb. Use fine-grit sandpaper to keep them under control. The thicker they get, the more likely they are to dry, split, and become painful and infected.

To develop your confidence in making spares, play this game:

- **Frame 1** Deliver one ball for a strike.: Score 10 points for success, otherwise 0.
- **Frame 2** Deliver two balls to knock down nine pins. Score 10 points for success, otherwise 0.
- **Frame 3** Deliver two balls to knock down eight pins. Score 20 points for success; otherwise 0.
- **Frame 4** Deliver two balls to knock down seven pins. Score 20 points for success, otherwise, 0.
- **Frame 5** Deliver two balls to knock down six pins. Score 30 points for success, otherwise 0.
- **Frame 6** Deliver two balls to knock down five pins. Score 30 points for success, otherwise 0.
- **Frame 7** Deliver two balls to knock down four pins. Score 40 points for success, otherwise 0.

- **Frame 8** Deliver two balls to knock down three pins. Score 40 points for success, otherwise 0.
- **Frame 9** Deliver two balls to knock down two pins. Score 50 points for success, otherwise 0.
- **Frame 10** Deliver one ball to knock down one pin. Score 50 points for success, otherwise 0.

Be a gracious winner and an even more gracious loser. A good bowler is, above all else, a good sportsman or sportswoman. No matter what the outcome, enjoy the game.

Do not equate individual scores with ability. Bowling is funny that way—it's possible to bowl well and score terribly. It's also possible to bowl terribly and score well. What matters most is your average over a period of time and on various lane conditions. Good technique improves both your high scores and your low scores. This is what raises your average.

Bowling apparel should be cool, comfortable, and non-binding. Only your shoes should be snug, to provide safe, secure, and consistent footing.

Learn the rules of the game. They are readily available from a variety of sources. League rules may vary from sanctioned rules.

When two bowlers step up to the approach at the same time, the person on the right goes first. That person may defer by simply taking a step back.

Always pick up your ball with both hands placed on the sides of the ball. Never put your hands in line with other balls on the return. Doing so risks serious injury.

Never complain about the lane conditions; they are the same for everyone. A bowler reads and adjusts to the lane conditions. That's what bowling is really all about. Let your opponent complain about the conditions. It's an excuse used for losing.

"If you keep doing what you've always done, you'll just keep getting what you've always gotten."—author unknown

An old bowling adage is "Make your spares and the strikes will take care of themselves." This is the same as saying that it is okay to roll a bad first shot as long as you have the skill to make spares. *It is NOT okay to roll a bad first shot.* If you do so consistently, it means that you lack the skill to make spares consistently. A better motto is "Learn to hit the pocket with the first shot. You will get plenty of strikes, and the spares you have to make will be easy ones." The **SPARE** system allows you to do exactly that.

Never lose your temper when you make a bad shot. The ball is telling you something and you need to pay attention to it. Remember universal truth number 2: You cause what the ball does. Diagnose the shot, figure out what went wrong, correct your technique with an adjustment, and move on. Keep in mind that a practice session is absolutely worthless if you don't learn something. Now that you know how to bowl, every shot you make is a practice session.

Keep food and drinks behind the bowling area. Anything on the floor will be stepped on. That person will then track it up onto the approach where it will cause problems for everybody, including the risk of serious injuries that can result from falling with a heavy ball in your hands.

🎳 Do not waste time up on the approach. Get into your stance, do a quick checklist, and go. Other people are waiting to bowl also.

🎳 Your target does not need to be an arrow. It can be any board in the area of the arrows.

🎳 Use the heaviest ball you can manage reliably. The more a ball weighs, the less it will deflect when it strikes the pins. You want the ball to drive through the pins in order to create effective action.

🎳 For the best chance of a strike, the ball should enter the pocket heading directly for the five pin. This rule of thumb is the reason this pin is referred to as the kingpin.

🎳 No combination of pins can be properly referred to as a split if the head pin is among them.

🎳 Do not store your bowling ball in your car during cold weather. Cold hardens the ball's cover, making it slide farther down the lane. It will act inconsistently as its temperature changes. Also, moisture will condense on any surface colder than the surrounding air. You will have to deal with that as well. A cold ball all but guarantees that you will have a bad night.

🎳 League bowlers are classified according to their averages. Your average is a function of many basic elements. Among them are:

1. Passion for the game
2. Education about the game
3. Physical ability
4. Experience
5. Lane conditions where you bowl
6. The nature of your equipment

🎳 "Learn how to keep score!"—Carol Mancini, *California Bowling News*

🎳 Hook is a double-edged sword. On one side, it increases the size of your strike zone. On the other side, balls that hook a lot create some godawful-looking spares.

🎳 If you find yourself missing a lot of corner pins because your ball is hooking too much, try using a "house ball" to make these spares. They generally hook much less.

🎳 You have the right to expect only one lane on each side of you to be clear before you bowl. Waiting for more space delays play for everyone.

🎳 "A thumbhole can never be too big." Ray Smith, former professional bowler out of Erie, Pennsylvania, on how to keep a ball from hanging up on your hand.

🎳 "Every lane has a line to the pocket. Your job is to find it, then stay on it all night long." Luke Curlett, bowler extraordinaire.

To determine the proper distance from the foul line for you to begin your approach, place your heels at the foul line with your back facing the pins. Without actually using a bowling ball, perform your normal approach, then turn around. This will be your starting point.

Afterword

Many books, manuals, pamphlets, and magazine articles have been written to teach the art of bowling. Where these resources fall short is that they teach technique but little else. Bowling is as much a *mental* game as it is a *physical* one.

The Essentials of Bowling arms you with knowledge gained over forty years of league, tournament, and coaching experience, boiled down into techniques that actually work that take less than one page to list. It explains *why* these techniques work. It teaches you how to physically practice the perfect game without even going to a bowling establishment.

It also teaches you a thought pattern. Teaching what to think about, as well as what to do, is what makes this book unique. Combining the physical and mental aspects of the game leads to repeatable performance, which is the key to success. The instructions, tips, and secrets revealed in this book will enable you to train yourself to bowl like a champion. If you are new to this game, I envy you. I wish someone had given me a copy of this book forty years ago.

Now quit making excuses and get to work. Remember: that fifteen feet of approach is your stage; and you want to put on a good show.

Appendix

🎳 A tenpin is 15 inches tall and can weigh anywhere from 3 lb. 4 oz. to 3 lb. 10 oz.

🎳 A bowling ball is 27 inches in circumference and can weigh up to 16 lb. There is no minimum weight.

🎳 The illustration on the opposite page shows the dimensions of a typical bowling alley.

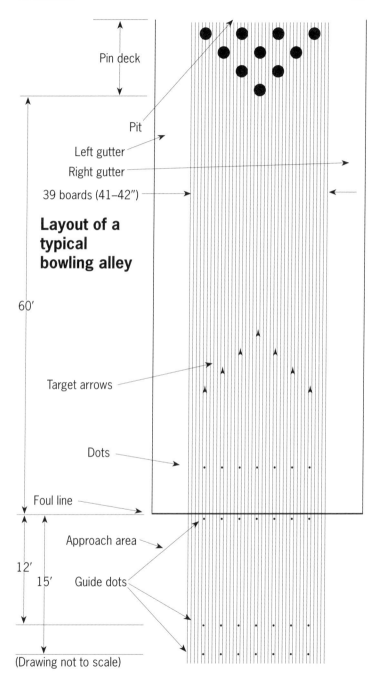

Pin deck

Pit

Left gutter

Right gutter

39 boards (41–42")

Layout of a typical bowling alley

60'

Target arrows

Dots

Foul line

Approach area

12'

15'   Guide dots

(Drawing not to scale)

Order additional copies

Do you know a bowler who could benefit from the instructions in this manual? *The Essentials of Bowling* makes an ideal gift for any occasion. To order additional copies, enclose a check or money order payable to:

> King Pin Publishing
> P.O. Box 22
> Fairview, Pennsylvania 16415

Pricing is as follows:

> $13.95 per copy (available in softcover only)
> $5.35 S&H (this will cover up to five copies)

Add $2.00 per book for signed copies (proceeds to support junior bowling programs).

All orders will be shipped within three days of receipt.

Pricing guarantee expires December 31, 2013.